FIRESIDE FOLKLORE OF WEST VIRGINIA VOL. 4

SHERRI BRAKE

FIRESIDE FOLKLORE OF WEST VIRGINIA VOL. 4

DEDICATION

For Dad

In every life, there are those that inspire us, encourage us to do better and believe in us. This book is dedicated to my dad, Larry Brake. Born and raised in Webster Springs, West Virginia, he grew up in the very best of the "old days" as he often reminisced. He was an avid family genealogist and historian, a lover of music, a photographer, a family man and when it came down to it, he was just one cool dude.
See ya' on the other side.

CONTENTS

ACKNOWLEDGMENTS

With the writing and conclusion of this series of four books on West Virginia folklore, I would like to acknowledge and thank those who submitted their experiences, photographs and stories to me over the course of this series. Folklore, ghosts and dark history continue to gain popularity in the mainstream but many of us have loved these subjects long before they became popular on television and in society.

CHAPTER 1

THE SILVER DOLLAR PLANT

Money doesn't grown on trees....but......

I was nine years old when I first saw this unique plant and I have never come across one like it since that day. I am sure there are many fields full of this plant, but I have never been lucky enough to see them.

I recall we were visiting family in Lost Creek, West Virginia for the weekend. We had driven down from our home in northeast Ohio to see my aunt, uncle, and my two cousins. They had bought an old, white farmhouse in Harrison County with a wraparound porch and a tree swing and we were anxious to see it. The big, old house sat amongst large trees and on the side of a sloping hill above a flowing creek. I recall hearing the words *Lost Creek* and I remember being puzzled because as far as I was concerned, the creek was 'found' and running through my cousins front yard!

Cousin's House
Lost Creek, West Virginia
Photo by the author

The next morning of our visit, my aunt packed all of us kids into the trusty station wagon and drove us into town to see her friend for a visit. I remember it was a sunny afternoon and as kids tend to do, we headed outside and into the yard to play and explore. It was at that time that I came across the most unusual looking plant. I remember picking up several of the fallen pods and could not help but notice how bizarre they looked. They were flat, white and oval shaped and they looked like a white silver dollar. My aunt had come outside with her friend and had exclaimed that we had found the money tree. She told us we could take a couple dollars and plant them and perhaps we could have our very own money tree one day. I was devastated a week later to discover that my money plant seeds had gone through the wash and were shredded. Since that day back in 1972, I have thought about that money plant and wondered why I have never seen once since then.

Money Plant
Photo by the author

As I grew older, I developed a love of gardening and planted trees, flowers and herbs when possible. I never saw the Silver Dollar plant advertised in seed catalogs or at local nurseries...no matter how often I looked. After doing some research, I found out many regarded my treasured plant as a weed. I also found out that the Pilgrims brought the Silver Dollar plant to the colonies on the Mayflower. Thomas Jefferson grew them in the famous gardens of his beloved Monticello and mentioned them in his letters. Today, if you look up money plant care, instructions are difficult to find. The plants originally hailed from Europe and were one of the first flowers grown in the gardens of the New World.

Silver Dollar plants consist of a variety of herbaceous perennials that reach heights of two to three feet and spreads of one to two feet. The flowering plant yields purple blossoms, although the Silver Dollar is most well-known for its large, flat seedpods that are often dried and sold commercially. The plant produces large, heart-shaped leaves during its first growth cycle and develops the large, purple or magenta blooms the second and subsequent seasons.

Seedpods
Photo by the author

They are members of the family *Brassicaceae* or mustard family. The Silver Dollar plant is often called the *Honesty* plant because the name *honesty* refers to the frankness in displaying its seeds so openly in their pods.

The plants various uses can be found in old folklore and wives tales. Various folk cultures and traditions assign symbolic meanings to plants. Although these are no longer commonly understood by populations that are increasingly divorced from their old rural traditions, some survive. In addition, these meanings are alluded to in older pictures, songs and writings. Back in the hills and hollers of Appalachia, the plant was often used for charms and potions by so-called Granny Witches who believed the plant would bring prosperity. I cannot wait to find one and place it in my garden in a special place of honor. It is a perfect blend of beauty, nature, and folklore.

Silver dollar plant, draw money now to me-
Under a full moon so bright, please bless me with prosperity.

CHAPTER 2

THE LOST SOUL OF LOST RIVER

Lost River State Park. Even the name of the park suggests a bit of mystery and intrigue. Doesn't it? This West Virginia state park is located in a heavily wooded area of Hardy County and near the town of Mathias. It sits on the land acquired in 1796 by "Light Horse" Henry Lee. He was a noted Revolutionary War hero and father to Confederate General Robert E. Lee who gained notoriety during the War Between the States. Due to overwhelming debt, Henry Lee sold the land off in 1809.

Lee's son, Charles Carter Lee, began re-acquiring his father's land around 1840 with the intent to build a resort hotel. Charles was quite the entrepreneur and desired to cater to visitors who

were intrigued with the nearby mineral springs. The salt sulphur
water was believed to have therapeutic healing qualities. Several
cabins were being constructed at that time but the work on the
main hotel resort did not begin until 1848. Before the hotel was
opened and functioning, the land and one of the cabins would
become a location immersed in dark history. The two story frame
and hand-hewn log structure is known as the Lee cabin. It sits
among ancient pine trees and in a mountainous glen. The beauty
of the pastoral setting belies its violent past.

Vintage Post Card of a Cabin at Lost River State Park

Our tale of murder takes us back to a livestock trader from Mt
Jackson, Virginia. Charles Sager had headed his cattle over the
mountains and made the nearly forty-mile trip to Moorefield to
sell his stock. The trip turned out to be very profitable but his
streak of good luck was about to take a sudden turn for the
worse. Several men ambushed him from a secluded spot on the
Moorfield Mountain Road. The robbers drug Sager thru the woods
and took him into the secluded Lee cabin. After torturing him for

a while, they violently stabbed him to death. When found much later, his body was laying in the corner of the room and up against the wall on the second floor. Dark stains of blood could easily be seen as it had greatly pooled around him before running down thru the floorboards and along the wall. The violence of the deed was evident and those that found him were undoubtedly shocked by the violence of the crime.

A serene view typical of the area at Lost River State Park.
Photo by the author 2008

The Lee cabin still stands today as part of the Lost River property which opened as a state park in 1937. The cabin now serves as a museum. There are four rooms inside the cabin and interesting enough, the walls upstairs are whitewashed with paint. Legend has it that the bloodstains could never be erased and the paint was an easy solution.

Photo by Justin A. Wilcox 2014
Wikimedia Commons image

Several ghost stories and a couple of actual paranormal events have occurred at or near the cabin. Some investigators claim to have captured wispy ectomist in their photographs. People say the ghost of Charles Sager is possibly seeking acknowledgment of his violent murder. The resort that was built there burnt to the ground in 1923. A few visitors claimed to hear ghostly screams from the woods over by the cabin. The owner of the resort at that time was a Mr Carr. He was widowed and was ready for his marriage to his second wife when his resort burned to the ground- on his wedding day. Some speculated and said it may have been the result of the first wife's ghost while others claimed it to be the ghost of old Sager. Some Park Rangers may tell you of this haunted history and some may laugh and mark it up to vivid imaginations. The truth is only known by poor Charles Sager and his killers.

Dark history aside, to visit this location is a true treat. Located in the wooded mountains of Hardy County in West Virginia, this state park offers cabin lodging and an abundance of outdoor recreation with plenty of room to roam. There many trails to explore as over three thousand acres make up this state park in the Eastern Panhandle. Lost River is known for its Cranny Crow overlook on top of Big Ridge Mountain, which offers a commanding view of five counties.

CHAPTER 3

GHOSTLY HITCHIKERS
APPARITION EXPEDITION

These ghostly travelers are found in folklore and ghost stories across the globe dating back to the days of traveling by horseback. Today, these entities are seen by unsuspecting motorists as they traverse their miles by motorized vehicles instead of horse and cart. These spectral hitchhikers have been viewed along city streets, deserted highways and vacant, curvy back roads. Most of the time the event occurs in the evening or late at night, many times while drivers are traveling solo. You never know when it may happen to you but one thing is for certain, it will leave you puzzled and certainly doubting your vision and perhaps your sanity.

Phantom hitchhikers; the mere description can cause the solo traveler to become uneasy. What it is about a ghostly walker at night that makes us so leery? Most tend to vaporize into thin air with no harm being done to the driver. Many reports tend to happen in the same location and feature the same subject such as the one that occurs just outside of Elkins, West Virginia.

Along a certain stretch of road, the young girl appears to be alone and a bit forlorn looking. She sits near a bridge and upon a large stone. Many drivers stop to offer her aid that she readily accepts. She remains silent but gives the address of her home, which is in the city limits of Elkins proper. When the driver turns to ask the girl the address again, the girl has vanished seemingly into thin air. Some drivers remember the address and a few have actually stopped and knocked on the door to inquire about the little girl. On one instance, a gray haired woman is said to have told the driver that a young girl in the family was killed in a car accident many years ago. Of course, this is probably where urban legend enters our little ghost story, as it is difficult to prove this occurred without tracking down the driver. Nonetheless, it has occurred to a few drivers and worth the retelling. She is known locally as the Phantom Hitchhiker of US 33. The stretch of the road that is described in this tale has changed through the years as the road itself has changed. CR 151 is the correct location of the stretch of road, which runs between Belington and Elkins and near Dead Man's Curve.

Another unusual sighting is that of a dark clothed figure is that which has occurs south of Summersville and on US Route 19. The figure tends to walk on the south side of the road and seems to disappear into thin air as you drive past. On studying this unusual sighting, I spoke with several who had sighted the entity. All commented on the fact that it was a male and he was tall and was outfitted in dark clothing. Locals have told me of a horrific car accident that occurred near this section of road. Could this be one of the lost souls tied to this highway misfortune?

West Virginia Turnpike near Beckley in 1977
Wikimedia Commons image

The West Virginia Turnpike between Princeton and Charleston has been plagued with many paranormal happenings from UFO sightings to phantom hitchhikers. It was reported that a few old family cemeteries were moved in the construction of the highway and at least five workers died during its creation between 1952 and 1954. The highway runs along the sites of several major floods and unfortunate mine disasters. Due to lives lost in construction and the great difficulty in engineering, it has also been referred to as "Eighty-Eight Miles of Miracles." Most of the unusual spirited activity seems concentrated on a fifteen-mile stretch between the community of Mossy and the city of Beckley. Interestingly enough, two West Virginia State Troopers figure into the phantom hitchhiker reports. The story goes that a young girl was picked up as she apparently was wandering aimlessly along the highway. After being put safely into the back of the cruiser, she apparently disappeared into thin air. One hitchhiker, a young man, was arrested and put into the back of the trooper's car and when the trooper turned around, the man was gone and his handcuffs were lying on the seat. Quite puzzling to the trooper, I would imagine.

The most popular Phantom Hitchhiker in America would be Resurrection Mary. Mary has been seen outside of Chicago by quite a few travelers. Mary's story has graced documentaries, a movie and even a song. Since the 1930's, several men driving along Archer Avenue near Resurrection Cemetery have reported picking up a young woman hitchhiker. This young lady is dressed a bit formally in a white party dress and sits quietly. When the driver nears the Resurrection Cemetery, the young woman asks to be let out, whereupon she disappears into the cemetery.

Who or what are these solo ghostly hitchhikers-we do not know. What I CAN guarantee is that if it happens to you...well....consider yourself forewarned. And besides, didn't your mother warn you about picking up hitchhikers?

CHAPTER 4

THE THREE CROSSES

His name is not nearly as popular as his three crosses, which can be seen by the hundreds scattered across many states, along highways, farmland and scenic two lane backroads. His name was Bernard Coffindaffer and he came from a humble beginning. Born in January of 1935 to German immigrants who had come to West Virginia, he was a man on a mission from early on. After making millions in the coalmine industry, he had a spiritual vision. His heavenly visions told him to erect these crosses "for the Glory of Jesus Christ". Some called him crazy; others hailed him as a soldier of God. He was a Methodist minister and a World War II veteran.

Mr. Coffindaffer said in a 1991 interview that a spirit appeared to him after open-heart surgery in 1982 and told him to begin erecting the crosses in as many locations as he could. "The crosses are to remind people to remember that Jesus was crucified on a cross at Calvary for our sins, and He will soon return," he said. Mr Coffindaffer offered in another interview that he had built his cross clusters in twenty-nine states, the Philippines and Zambia. The first trio of crosses, which stood twenty-five feet high, was erected in 1984 about sixty-five miles north of Charleston. At last official count, he had erected one thousand, eight hundred and sixty-seven crosses, overall.

Central West Virginia Crosses
Photo by the author

You see them everywhere, on hillsides, in farm fields and along the highway. The first trio of crosses was erected in Flatwoods, West Virginia. Bernard's crosses consist of three crosses with the two shorter on the outside flanking the tallest one which stands in the center. The center cross is typically twenty-five feet in height with the shorter ones reaching about twenty feet. Most are similar in paint colors with the center one being gold and the outside crosses bearing a coat of pale blue. The gold paint on the center cross represented royalty while the two crosses' pale blue paint is said to represent the earth. At the erection of each cluster of crosses, a solemn service was held sharing the spirit and light of religion. As the years have passed, many crosses are well maintained by property owners while others have begun to splinter and the paint is showing age with fading and peeling.

Herold Road Crosses on US Route 19
Photo by the author

Bernard was the subject of a PBS documentary on his life entitled, "Point Man for God," and was shown on the award-winning series "Different Drummer." His popularity even garnered him a segment on CBS News. This worldly yet down to earth man was moved by his other worldly vision. His efforts still stand proudly along the roads of this nation and on private property as well. Every time I pass a trio of the crosses along the road, I cannot help but think of his passion and spirit.

This businessman turned evangelist died at his home in Craigsville back in 1993 and left a legacy of hope, enlightenment and a bit of controversy behind. It is estimated that he spent around three million dollars erecting his crosses. His obituary ran in the NY Times and shared his story with millions of curious people. For such a world traveler, he lies buried on a quiet hillside in the West Virginia Memorial Gardens in Calvin, just a few miles away from where I live.

Photo by the author

CHAPTER 5

CANYON CREATURE

The Blackwater River flows for thirty-two miles and as it passes the town of Davis, it flows over Blackwater Falls and into an eight-mile long canyon that is heavily wooded. It was here in this canyon in 1960 that a group of campers encountered a terrifying scene. One of the campers was cutting wood in preparation for the evening campfire when he felt a poke in his ribs. He heard a noise at the same time and turned thinking it was one of his fellow campers. Instead of seeing the face of a friendly camper as was to be expected, a large "horrible monster" leered back. The creature was seen by the other campers as well. It lumbered off into the shadows of the forest as the campers looked on in complete shock and fear. They stayed at the campsite for the rest of the night and I imagine they did *not* sleep well. The campers left early the next morning noting large footprints on the ground where the creature had been seen. The later said they were too frightened to follow the footprints. Can you blame them? The creature was described in detail later on by the campers, "it had two huge eyes that shone like big balls of fire and we had no light at all. It seemed every bit of eight feet tall and it had shaggy long hair all over its body. It just stood and stared at us. Its eyes were very far apart."

Vintage Woodcut of Werewolf-Like Creature

Unusual animal sightings have dotted folklore and historical record in the state dating back to when it was part of Virginia. Native American Indian folklore also speaks of these unusual elusive creatures that are large in size and typically covered in hair. In Parsons, just seventeen miles from Davis, another report of a monster-like creature was told in the summer of 1960. Were these just figments of over lively imaginations or an actual sighting of some kind of Bigfoot or Werewolf type creature? Cryptids have been defined as an animal claimed to exist, but for which there is no type specimen or formal description. When we think of Cryptids, the most famous in the Mountain State would undoubtedly be the Mothman.

Near Davis, West Virginia
Photo by the author

I consulted the Bigfoot Field Researchers Organizations (BFRO) and was intrigued to find four documented sightings posted for Tucker County in the database. The earliest *documented* sighting was in 1987 with the most recent occurring in 2008. All sightings had similar details with the description of the creature that was spotted. It really does make you wonder....

Blackwater River Canyon Overlook
Photo by Carson Maynard Wikimedia Commons

As we slowly encroach upon remote territory with campers, mountain bikers, spelunkers and adventurists, I imagine that sightings will continue to increase, intrigue and mystify. Perhaps one day we will have the answers that certain cryptids *do* exist. Until then, it makes for great, spooky stories around the summer campfire. Unless you were one of those campers in the canyon, of course.

CHAPTER 6

MEN IN BLACK

In honor of West Virginia's most unusual festival, The Mothman Festival, I thought I would touch on one aspect of the legends circulated at Point Pleasant. The elusive Men in Black (MIB) were the subject of great study by Gray Barker. Mr Barker was an American writer best known for his books about paranormal phenomena and UFOs and Barker was noted for his dramatic style blurring fact with fiction to capture the imagination. His 1956 book *They Knew Too Much About Flying Saucers* introduced the notion of the Men in Black to UFO folklore. . The controversial book came out in 1956 when Eisenhower was president, Elvis Presley got his first gold album and the musical My Fair Lady was on Broadway. His book drew great attention and scrutiny as UFOs were in the news with sightings occurring across the state, in America and all over the entire world for that fact. The most popular UFO reporting in the state would be the infamous Flatwoods Green Monster sighting in September of 1952.

Exactly what are these Men in Black? These men dressed in black suits and claimed to be government agents who would harass and occasionally threaten UFO witnesses to keep them quiet about what they have seen. These sightings and visitations began back in the 1950s and even continue today according to many conspiracy theorists and ufologists. The Men in Black are mentioned in various folklore, movies, books and in music with the band Blue Öyster Cult directly mention the MIB in the lyrics of two of their songs. In 1957, Author John Keel, gave an account of alleged sightings of a gigantic winged creature called Mothman in the vicinity of Point Pleasant during 1966 and 1967 and mentions the MIB as part of the frightening and incredulous storyline.

The Saucerian Magazine/ November 1953

Sightings of these mysterious men in dark clothing were the singular events that would inspire the Tommy Lee Jones and Will Smith movies of the same name.

Mpthman Statue in Point Pleasant, West Virginia
Photo by author 2017

Pop culture movies such as *The Matrix* played off this theme as well to a certain extent. Some people now say that Gray Barker's story was merely that...a story and some go as far to call it a fascinating hoax. As many of you know, with every piece of folklore, there is usually a nugget of truth in the tale somewhere. Mr Barker was an editor for a UFO themed magazine, which he suddenly shut down after a visit from government officials dressed in black suits. (Go figure.)

In 1947, a man by the name of Harold Dahl, claimed to have been warned not to talk about his alleged UFO sighting that occurred on Maury Island in Puget Sound in Washington State. This sighting took place before the Roswell Incident but bore a few similarities. Dahl said he was warned by a man in a dark suit to not speak about his sighting.

In the mid-1950s, the ufologist, Albert K. Bender claimed he was visited by men in dark suits who threatened and warned him not to continue investigating UFOs. Bender maintained that the Men in Black were secret government agents who had been given the task of suppressing evidence of UFOs. Sound familiar?

Folklorist James R. Lewis compares accounts of men in black with tales of people encountering Lucifer and speculates that they can be considered a kind of "psychological drama." Whether these original sightings are actual facts or science fiction, Men in Black continue to be reported in rare instances across the world.

Beam me up, Scotty.

CHAPTER 7

DARK AS A DUNGEON
COAL MINING GHOSTS

'I hope when I'm dead and the ages shall roll
That my body will blacken and turn into coal
I will look from the door of my heavenly home
And pity the miner a' diggin' my bones'

Merle Travis

He told me about his experiences deep in the mine over the phone. As he spoke, goosebumps formed on both of my arms and on the back of my neck. He had started our phone call with the words, "I am a God fearin' man." He then began to relate to me some of the unusual happenings that had been occurring deep in the mine he worked at which was in southern West Virginia. Odd experiences and unexplainable visual apparitions were beginning to take a toll on many of the workers. (Especially on the God fearing man who was strong enough to call a complete stranger for help.) I sat intently as he spoke about his many years of working this particular deep mine.

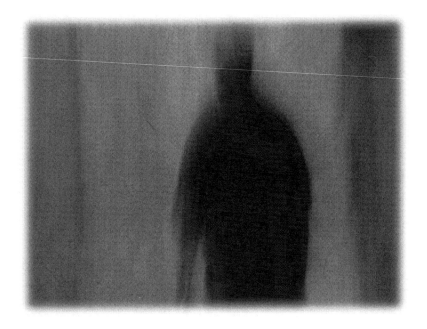

A sketch showing a type of Shadowman

"Some of the guys are seeing it" he told me. "It's not just me. This thing, this weird thing is big. It almost looks like a large black trash bag over a big man. It streaks across the side of the mine and just out of your vision a little bit and then it disappears, poof!! This thing moves fast-real fast. Its startles a man, ya know?" I assured him that I knew all too well about shadow people. I was pretty sure this was the phenomena he and other miners were experiencing. Shadow People or Shadow Men are a type of paranormal phenomena that evades explanation. Many researchers believe it to be a type of energy some believe it to be dark energy and other believe it to be the Djinn, which is pronounced as 'gin'. Djinn are believed to exist in a parallel dimension in the physical world. They are "here" but in a place that we typically cannot see or experience. Some would call them Shape Shifters. These shadowy forms can be male, female and of any size. They can also be in the shape of an animal. My first impression was that this is the type of entity being seen at this particular mine.

Beckley, West Virginia Coal Miner Statue
Photo by the author

More on the subject of shadow people. Djinn are also mentioned in various cultures across the world. Muslim mythology includes angels and the spirits known as djinns, which are described in the Qur'an as being able to interact with people despite being made of a "smokeless fire." Djinns are known for having free will, and for being either good or evil, like humans. The word djinn comes from the Arabic jinn, a plural noun that means both "demons or spirits" and also, literally, "hidden from sight."

Sketch of a Typical Shadowman
Artist credit to Timitzer

My caller went on to explain that various coal mining equipment would turn itself on. He explained that some of the equipment had several steps that needed to be done before it could be turned on-that it was not a simple switch that was turned to start. He also told me that often he would see this shadowy thing right before equipment would turn on. I can only imagine how frightening this would be. My caller also told me he had heard his name whispered right next to his ear....when no one else was around him. Often he would find himself in an older part of the mine removing something off an old piece of equipment that was not working anymore to place on other equipment somewhere else in the mine. It was at these times when "things" would happen to him. Others experienced the same thing as well but many men were reluctant to speak of them. Many were surprised when they eventually confided in each other as the same experiences were happening to many of the miners.

Bolt Mountain area
Photo by author 2010

As our call started to wrap up, I asked if it was possible for me to visit the mine site. I wanted to go down to where it all was happening and investigate it for myself. Maybe I could help get the spirits to rest easier. I could at least try, right? My caller told me that it would be almost impossible for me to do that. Lots of rules and regulations and of course, if we were caught, he could lose his job. And didn't I know about the old miner's superstition? To have a woman's shadow cast over the entrance to a mine was bad luck, he told me. Some of the older workers may get troubled if they knew I was there at the mine.

My further research on the Bolt Mountain area was interesting but did not turn up much. Bolt was named for postmaster George Washington Bolt, who was born in 1864 and passed in 1943. Being a fan of country music, I was surprised to see that Grand Ol' Opry star and singer, Little Jimmy Dickens, was born at Bolt in 1920.

Crossing West Virginia Route 99, both over and through Bolt Mountain, is not for the faint of heart or amateur first time driver. First paved in the 1960s, the steep and sloped route serves both coal truck and timber drivers and local residents of parts of Boone, Wyoming and Raleigh counties. With most of the area being forested and rural, it came to no surprise that various sightings of unusual animals have come to light during research. Reports of Bigfoot type creatures and fast moving white animals were evidenced in my research of the area as well an occasional reference to a Bolt Mountain Monster.

Even though it is remote, crime finds its way into every hill and holler. A Caucasian woman's skeleton that was discovered on Bolt Mountain in 1993. Two Wyoming County men were hunting on the mountain when they noticed a white object lying on the ground. One of the men went down to have a look and kicked it and saw that he'd uncovered a partial human skull. As of the writing of this book, the case is still not solved on whose remains were discovered.

Bolt Mountain; even its name causes you to picture a striking landscape in your mind. Mountains have always held a special place in the soul of man. From the beginning of time, humankind has been fascinated with mountains. Why do mountains touch the human spirit? Is it their solitude and isolation? Is it their shear mass? The ancients believed that mountains formed the foundation of the world, that mountains surround the world and provide a resting place for the firmament (an inverted, transparent bowl separating the heavens from the earth), and that gods ruled from the top of mountains. Seeing Bolt Mountain and surrounding peaks rise from a foggy mist, I would tend to agree.

I often think of that miner who called me and wonder if the spirits have settled down deep in that mountain mine. Perhaps they found peace at last, we can only hope.

CHAPTER 8

THE ASYLUM CEMETERY

To be laid to rest in peace. It conjures up mental imagery of manicured lawns, nicely decorated headstones and beautiful flowers. This is not always the case in most institution burial grounds. Neglect can be prevalent, not due to uncaring, but more due to the lack of funds for upkeep, I imagine. I have seen prison cemeteries with waist high weeds and metal markers for headstones bearing only the inmates name and death date. At the old Weston State Hospital, the case is pretty much the same except no markers can be found, save but for a few.

Patients who died at the asylum sometimes stayed there. Perhaps I should rephrase that and say that their bodies stayed. Many patients simply had no living relatives to claim them or if they did have family they were either too ashamed to come forward or lived too far away. It would be difficult to travel to Weston to retrieve their remains for burial near the family home, especially back before motorized travel. On occasion, a traveling hobo or transient worker could be committed, sometimes just for public drunkenness, and he would never leave. The asylum provided burial with a minimum of ceremony and display, though there are accounts of doctors and staff attending services.

Cover of an old Weston Hospital publication

Looking thru what burial records are available for the asylum provides you an assortment of various causes of death. Everything from Apoplexy, tuberculosis, breast cancer, gangrene paresis, syphilis and exhaustions is listed. Suicides are noted such as Peter Morris on November 12 of 1892. Peter used a rope to end his apparently troubled life. Poor Gunther Scnell took his own life on August 21 of 1891 by strangulation, probably a rope, belt or sheet but no additional information is given.

Trans Allegheny Lunatic Asylum
Photo by the author 2013

The influenza epidemic claimed asylum patients such as John Murriskc. His cause of death was listed as influenza with his date of death as October 28, 1918. The influenza epidemic of 1917-18 moved with speed and was very fatal. Sometimes entire families would perish due to the communicable nature of this strain.

Other causes of death listed typical of an asylum were psychosis, manic depression, paralysis of insane, and mental defectives. Cancer is listed as the cause of death and is repeated often in the records with various types noted such as; pancreas, bladder, renal, stomach and even lip cancer.

A view of one of the cemeteries at the Asylum.
Photo by the author 2014

Unusual deaths noted were those of Mike Parfeniewtz on April 16, 1938 and his thirstiness for lye. Elvira Shaw perished when she had a "cutter accident" on December 21 of 1960. She was eighty-six when death knocked on her door. Neville Spinks simply fell out of bed and died on July 17 of 1957.

A Lone Grave Marker
Photo by the author 2014

As with any large institution, records are unfortunately misplaced due to human error, destroyed accidently or lost to fire. There are many that have survived and each one tells a story. Take the story of Anna Adkins. Anna O'Dell married Ison J. Adkins, who worked as a tanner, in 1891 in Roane Co., WV. At the time of her death, Anna was a widow and a patient at Weston State Hospital where she was committed for thirty years, one month and eleven days. She was a young woman of just eighteen years when she was first brought to Weston. Her death certificate reveals that her ultimate cause of death was tuberculosis. Anna was buried in the hospital cemetery in an unmarked grave after no one from her family came to claim her body.

Vincent Amos of Moundsville, West Virginia was fifty-two years old when he passed from encephalitis in 1955 after being a patient at the hospital for twelve years. He is interred in the hospital cemetery. A copy of his death certificate is seen below.

Monument Erected and Dedicated to the Memory of the Patients
Dedicated 1999
Photo by the author 2014

It is said that approximately 20,000 people died here between 1864 and the closing in 1994. Some sources state the number as much higher. As I strolled into the first cemetery, I saw a nice marker noting the cemetery. I knew that since many of these bodies were wards of the state, that an elaborate funeral and fancy coffin was highly unlikely. I have been to cemeteries like this before and realized that the dead were probably wrapped in blankets or placed in simple pine boxes.

As I looked about the vast cemetery, I wondered about the asylum patients. It seemed a beautiful setting for a cemetery with rolling hills and a view of the serene countryside.

I hope they are resting easy.

CHAPTER 9

THE LEGEND OF BELSNICKEL

Belsnickel. Years ago, the very mention of the word would cause nervousness and apprehension among some children in Germany, especially those who were mischievous or misbehaving in nature. In the 1750's in our Mountain State, immigrants from Germany arrived bringing with them their Christmas customs, one of which is the legend of Belsnickel. Many of these immigrants arrived and settled in what is now Berkeley, Greenbrier, Hardy and Pendleton counties.

Belsnickel was one of several companions of Saint Nicholas, a character who originated in the Rhine, which included Germany, Switzerland and France. He comes to children one to two weeks before Christmas, wearing old and tattered clothing adorned with raggedy fur. He is typically a rough and tumble looking character and appears to be cranky, for lack of a better term. Belsnickel carries a hickory switch or a stick to frighten children while bearing a pocketful of candy and nuts to reward them for good behavior. One by one, Belsnickel would call the children out and ask them to recite a Bible verse, a well-known poem or perhaps complete a math problem. If they could not complete the task that was asked of them, they would receive a slight tap on the back with the switch. Belsnickel's job was to remind the wee ones that they still had a little time left to behave before Saint Nicholas would arrive on Christmas.

Old German sketch of Belsnickel
Public Domain

The history of Belsnickel is intriguing. He was a popular Christmas character developed around the Middle Ages in European countries. Germany was known to have both happy and grim gift-bringers, and the Belsnickel was the very grim one. He was not only feared but also got children to behave nicely through the year so that they could receive gifts during Christmas.

Belsnickel is the first character in the history of Christmas characters who clearly distinguished between good children and bad children, unlike Santa Claus who presented gifts to those whose names were on the famous 'Santa's list'.

In modern day visits in areas that still celebrate the folklore of Belsnickel, the hickory switch is only used for noise of course and to warn children they still have time to be good before Christmas. Then *all* the children get candy (of course) if they are polite about it. The origin of the name? The name Belsnickel is a combination of the German word *belzen* (meaning to wallop) and *nickel* for St. Nicholas.

Call him the dark side of Santa, but Belsnickel's job was to remind wee ones that they still had a little time left to behave before Santa's official arrival on Christmas Eve. Maybe I am just getting older and a bit cranky myself, but it seems to me that many misbehaving kids of today could use a visit by Belsnickel to get them motivated for good behavior. I am sure many of you are in full agreement with me. Can you imagine a Belsnickel type Santa at your local mall before Christmas?

CHAPTER 10

THE WILD MAN OF CLAY COUNTY

Some stories do not need embellishment as the facts can be intriguing enough all by themselves. Such is the tale of the Wild Man of Clay County. It was 1908 and Henry Ford had just produced his Model T automobile in Michigan; President Taft was elected, Butch Cassidy and the Sundance Kid were killed and the Wild Man of Clay County was born. Orval was born to Sarah Elizabeth (Mitchell) Brown and husband John Logan Brown. He would live a life many envied...or at least were fascinated with.

Orval White often said that he was greatly influenced by Edgar Rice Borough's book *Tarzan of the Apes* and subsequently, the movie. Tarzan's character was described as being extremely athletic, handsome, tall and suntanned with wavy, long black hair. He was brave, smart and loyal to those he cared about... a great model for kids growing up in the Great Depression. A local newspaper column stated that Orval was an avid reader and enjoyed various outdoor pastimes and he loved to climb trees.

The Adventures of Tarzan by Edgar Rice Burroughs

While growing up in Clay County, Orval seemed to have an aversion to clothing- -befitting of any Tarzan admirer-- and preferred the outdoor country life. Life on the family farm surely became boring for a wanderlust soul such as his and with just seventeen years behind him and an 8th grade education, he left home for the open road making it as far as the Rio Grande...on foot he later claimed. After returning home a few years later, Orval donned a loincloth and posed for photographs charging twenty-five cents for each photo. He later claimed that on some days he made as much as thirty dollars posing with locals and out of towners who came in search of the countrified Tarzan. Occasionally he worked the fairs and carnivals dressed only in his loincloth and flexing his muscles. Thirty dollars a day? Not bad for a self-made Wild Man.

Local newspaper clipping of the Wild Man and a fan

In the 1940's Uncle Sam came calling and our Wild Man of Clay County served in the Army and then did a short stint in the Navy as well from 1941-1943. After an honorable Naval discharge, he returned home and it was there that his life took a violent and unexpected turn.

In the Beckley Post-Herald newspaper dated June 13 1951, it stated that Orval Brown, age 53, was deemed insane in regards to the murder of his cousin and ordered to be committed to the old Weston State Hospital. (Now known as the Trans-Allegheny Lunatic Asylum) Wilford Reedy, a first cousin to Orval, was killed. "He was comin' at me with an axe, I had to shoot him. He was drunk, a regular outlaw," he said. Regardless of his self-defense statement, he was convicted and sent to Weston where he lived for seventeen years. After his discharge from the asylum in 1968, he returned to Clay County. Eventually, his health began to decline and he passed away in 2005 at the ripe old age of ninety-eight years. He had outlived all four of his siblings. The wild man who claimed to live a clean life free from sex, drugs and alcohol is buried in the Brown Cemetery in Indore just a few miles from where he once ran free, played in caves, swung from backyard trees and flexed his muscles.

Sleep well, Mr. Wild Man.

CHAPTER 11

A GOLD DOME, A FIRE AND A COUPLE OF GHOSTS

I remember passing by the Capitol many times as a child while on road trips. On our vacation trips from NE Ohio to West Virginia, we would sometimes drive by on the highway and as we did, my parents would often tell us about the gold on the dome. You could always see the sun glinting and glistening off the gold-colored top and I was not sure if I really believed the story about it being gold, but it sure did make you wonder. What also tweaked my imagination were the Capitol House ghost sightings I heard about as a teenager.

The present capitol building in our state cost nearly ten million dollars to build. The reason I say "present" is a tongue in cheek reference to the fact that our state capitol switched back and forth a bit in the past from Wheeling to Charleston due to several factors. The architect was Cass Gilbert who was born in Zanesville, Ohio in 1859. In 1912, Gilbert designed the world's first skyscraper, the popular Woolworth Building in New York City. His beautiful capitol building in Charleston took almost ten years to complete on its north bank location on the Kanawha River.

Photo by the author in 2000

Tragedy struck the capitol on January 3, 1921 as billowing smoke was seen rising up from the top of the Capitol and soon thousands of spectators who stood in awe. They were soon treated to a rare display of fireworks, as thousands of rounds of ammunition exploded in the flames. The ammunition had been stock plied there because of the ongoing mine wars in the region. From the ashes of this fire soon rose a new building with multiple wings and a grand design.

The exterior of the massive classical-styled building is made from Indiana limestone. The dome stands nearly three hundred feet high and is seventy-five feet in diameter. The entire dome is gilded in 23 ½ karat gold leaf, which was applied to the copper and lead roof in tiny squares. My parents were right after all....it is gold!

The ghostly sightings I have heard about feature two apparitions. One is a woman who has been seen wandering the hallways before she disappears mysteriously. The other entity is a man who is dressed in maintenance clothing. His story is vague as well with most renditions saying he died from a heart attack on the job. If you are familiar with the paranormal and ghostly occurrences, it is believed that a job left unfished is cause enough for one to haunt. Perhaps this maintenance man felt tied to his earthly job enough to "hang around".

The capitol of West Virginia is a remarkable sight when the sun shines upon the golden dome. I can only wonder if those earthly ghosts know what a precious building they roam on their nightly spirited trek.

CHAPTER 12

The West Virginia Snallygaster

I know. You are already wondering just what in the world is a Snallygaster? Snallygaster is the name of the elusive flying reptilian that was originally spotted in Fredrick County, Maryland, and soon glided across state lines with sightings taking place in Ohio, Pennsylvania and West Virginia. With initial documentation beginning in the early 1900's you have to wonder was it due to multiple hallucinations, a concocted hoax to boost newspaper sales or was there something truly unusual going on out there?

Early folklore accounts describe the community in Maryland being terrorized by a monster called a Schneller Geist, meaning "quick ghost" in German. The earliest incarnations mixed the half-bird features of a siren with the nightmarish features of demons and ghouls. The Snallygaster was described as half-reptile, half-bird with a metallic beak lined with razor-sharp teeth, occasionally with octopus-like tentacles. It swoops silently from the sky to pick up and carry off its victims. The earliest stories claim that this monster sucked the blood of its victims. Seven-pointed stars, which reputedly kept the Snallygaster at bay, can still be seen painted on local barns in Maryland. In West Virginia….well…that is a different story.

Science has yet to prove the existence of the Snallygaster, which means this creature, is categorized as a cryptid, just like Bigfoot, Mothman and the slippery Loch Ness Monster in Scotland. I was surprised to see the word Snallygaster listed in the dictionary and was intrigued with its definition; *A mythical nocturnal creature that is reported chiefly from rural Maryland, is reputed to be part reptile and part bird, and is said to prey on poultry and small children.* Another source described the creatures loud howling as "blood curdling" before an apparent attack.

Sketch of a Snallygaster and Prey
Artist Unknown

The newspaper description of the creature would be enough to spark fear in even the sturdiest of mountain folk. It was described as having a long razor sharp beak, steel-like claws and a solo eye, just like a cyclops, in the center of its head. The stories spread rampant and far while coverage in local papers spurred its myth onwards. Near the town of Scrabble, it reportedly stalked a woman down causing great fear among her neighbors. Another sighting occurred in Franklin, which the *Pendleton Times* reported on with a local by the name of Kenneth Bland. Mr Bland was chased by the so-called Snallygaster and climbed up a tree to escape its steely claws. He sat there for hours out of fear as the creature disappeared as quickly as it had appeared. Bland was in shock apparently and did not want to take any chances with climbing down prematurely. Can you blame him?

In June of 1945, the town of Hopewell was the scene of multiple sightings. On June 29, a local town dog named 'Old Dog Blue', fell victim to the cyptid. Apparently, this was the only deaf dog in town as the other local dogs took off to hiding as soon as the heard the Snallygaster's horrific howling. The people hid and many cowered in their homes fearful for their livestock left outside. Poor Old Dog Blue.

In the Parkersburg area, a local who lived just south of town in 1946, told neighbors of the death of some of his chickens. Bodies were mutilated and strewn about his farm as if a giant creature had run wild tearing wing from fowl and not even damaging the fence, which surrounded his chickens and their coop. Just a few weeks later in Doddridge County, a coon hunter captured what he thought to be a Snallygaster cub. The report stated it was half the size of a rat and had the claws of a cat. It was thought to have been given to two local professors at Salem College but no news of this can be found.

What of the Snallygaster today? Sightings in the Mountain State continued into the 1970s but like any good cryptid story, what is fact and what is *legend* have become a bit blurred. I asked a cryptid researcher on the phone recently what he thought of the Snallygaster and as he paused, he laughed and said, "He and Mothman are probably hanging out in Vegas."

CHAPTER 13

See the Unbelievable Mystery Hole!

You can find a few of these scattered across the United States. These are places where time, distance and perception seem to shift a bit and the laws of gravity seem to be...well....warped. To some folks, it may harken back to the days of circus sideshows and sellers of snake oil. Do they exist? Are they real? Or maybe it just has to do with your imagination? Mystery Holes are intriguing and fascinating, as they seem to play with your vison and perception. My favorite one is in Fayette County and is on the old Midland Trail / Route 60.

From the outside, you take one look at the Quonset hut building with the Volkswagen beetle bug car sticking out of the side, and your first thought is WHAT IS THAT PLACE? *The Mystery Hole* definitely knows how to catch the eyes of passing motorists. A large black gorilla squats above the entrance while many U.S. flags blow proudly in the breeze from atop the building. A sign below proclaims proudly:

"An experience that will intrigue you the rest of your life."
"Nature's gravity seems to have gone haywire and your sense of balance is extremely upset."
"If your heart can take it, see the laws of nature defied."

Photo by the author 2011

I first visited the Mystery Hole back when I was a skinny, longhaired kid in the 1970's. Mom and dad stopped there on a trip thru the area and we kids were very excited to stop and shop and check it out for ourselves. It did not disappoint. Flash forward to my teen years and lo and behold, I just had to stop there again. Both times I just enjoyed it for what it was...a mystery. But now, with my most recent visit there being in my mid-forties, I took a wee bit longer to look around. I guess being an adult had made me more critical and questioning. Say, what makes that ball look like it can roll uphill by itself? Why does that water look like its flowing uphill? How does that tour guide stand there in that position and look like he's gonna fall over any minute? What the heck?

Photo by the author

Original owner Donald Wilson "discovered" its mysterious powers in 1972 and it was he who gave me my first tour into the *Mystery* of the Mystery Hole. A boisterous man, maybe a bit eccentric, but he had his speech down and was very entertaining. When Mr Wilson closed his attraction in 1996, he died soon afterward and the building sat empty for a while. Under new owners, it took on a new life and is open from May thru October to mystify and intrigue all who care to stop and pay admittance.

Friendly characters await you.
Photo by the author

The Mystery Hole is a quintessential and quirky roadside oddity and a classic throwback to the old days and simpler ways. Make a day of it and check out local Hawks Nest State Park, just two miles farther east with the New River Gorge Bridge just fifteen more miles away. If you get a chance, visit their website and take a drive over to experience the mystery for yourself. Pay your admission, be amazed and be sure to shop in the gift shop before you leave. Not a fan of the weird and whacky? The drive is beautiful and the experience will be memorable! www.mysteryhole.com

CHAPTER 14

Frontier Times in Summers County

The early settlers were self-sufficient, resilient people and if it had not been for their tenacity and bravery, we would not be here, of course. Clearing the land by hand (perhaps with the use of a horse or ox) was of foremost importance before building a cabin. Tending a garden and growing herbs for poultices and medicines, was as important as hunting and trapping for meat and fish. Combating disease back in the days before antibiotics, vaccines and good medical care was a feat unto itself. To make things even more dangerous, the threat of Indian attacks and retaliation was common and feared by all. The area where Summers County is located was the scene of great strife between the natives and the settlers.

Summers, the last county formed in the State, was created from Mercer, Monroe, Greenbrier and Fayette by act of February 27, 1871, and named from George W. Summers, who was born in Fayette County, Virginia, March 4, 1804, and accompanied his parents to the Kanawha Valley when but an infant. He attended school and graduated from Ohio University. He was a member of the Constitutional Convention of 1850, and the Whig candidate for Governor in 1851. In 1852, he was elected Judge of the Eighteenth Judicial Circuit of Virginia, but resigned in 1858. Nearly one hundred years prior to this, the area was fraught with Indian attacks and frontier violence.

Summers County Historical Signage
Photo by the author 2010

Various creeks and mountains bear names dating back to the violence of the era, such as Indian Creek. It was named this because of the Indian highway that meanders along the waterway and because of their camping ground at its mouth. Griffith's Creek was named after the old settler by the name of Griffith, who when a boy was kidnapped by the Indians and whose father was killed by them.

On October 19, 1763, there was a marauding band of thirty Shawnee braves that crossed the New River at the Mouth of Indian Creek and into the area known as Bradshaw and Spruce Run. It was there at what is known as Forest Hill, that Mr. Bradshaw, a settler from England, was captured by the Indians and horrifically burned at the stake. Not much is known of Mr. Bradshaw except for the fact that he was allegedly a pirate before settling in that area. He had laid claim to his land with a tomahawk claim in 1758 and supposedly buried some treasure in the vicinity, booty from his past pirating ventures.

Early Sketch of Chief Cornstalk
Wikicommons Media / Artist unknown

The Native Indians had discovered the footprints of Mr. Bradshaw as they had been on the river hunting. Following the trail, they ascended Indian Creek to the mouth of Bradshaw Run. Imagine such a sight! All bearing typical war paint and armed with bows and arrows with the exception of two who carrying rifles. After traveling up the creek for about a mile, they come to a small clearing with log cabin. It is there they discover our unlucky ex-pirate, Mr. Bradshaw. Legend says that they hid in the woods until they saw their victim coming to the spring for water. When the unsuspecting man is warned by a noise, the Indians shoot him to keep him from escaping. The wounded man starts to run only to be overtaken, captured and bound with ropes. They traveled on up the little run for about two miles where they stopped to camp and it was here they held a council. As they speak amongst themselves, they decide to condemn their captive to death by fire and it was this way that he was killed. Such was the life of the pioneer settlers as life was lived large and life was very fragile. White men and Indian alike, committed atrocities all in the name of survival. Very dangerous times on the frontier, indeed.

One of the Indians that were responsible for the capture of Mr. Bradshaw, came to be well known. You may have heard of him, as he was a great chief among the Shawnee. His Indian name was Hokoleskwa. The settlers called him Cornstalk and he became the prominent leader of the Shawnee nation just prior to the American Revolution. He was born about 1720 in what is now Western Pennsylvania. The Shawnee migrated to the Ohio Territory as they gave ground in the face of expanding American settlement. Cornstalk fought with the French against the British during the French and Indian War. Chief Cornstalk, the Great Chief, was murdered under a flag of truce in November of 1777, fourteen years after capturing Mr. Bradshaw.

CHAPTER 15

Red Rose: Memory of a Place and Time

"Motherhood:
All love begins and ends there."
--*Robert Browning*

One of the hardest days of my life was Friday, December 19 of 2014. The one person who knew me best and loved me unconditionally left this earth. When my mom passed away, it left a void in my life that at times is too painful to think about even now. She always told us kids, and there we three of us, if you talk about someone who has passed away and think of them often, you keep them alive by keeping their memory alive. All three of us daughters believe this and we hope that we are doing her proud by talking about her, thinking about her day in

64

and day out and by sharing her character and stories with others. This is one of those stories. It is in her own words as she wrote them and gave to me just two years before she left us.

In the 1970's I wanted to go back to my hometown. It was a little coal mining town at the end of a road that seemed to go nowhere. At the end of this road, there was a smaller dirt road leaving the little town and you could drive around the mountain and back up to the main highway. My husband and our small daughters were in the car with me. I could remember this town with only about ten homes in each row with a small road between them. There was a small school with two rooms, eight grades, a potbelly stove and a two-seater outhouse. There was also a very small company store where items were stocked out of a pickup truck. Outside stood a railroad tie with a line of mailboxes. Our laundry was always flopping in the breeze as it dried, even in the winter. We had chickens, blackberries and a garden, even the occasional copperhead snake, and my mother had the prettiest red rose bushes in town. It was always a treat to cut a branch to give to someone, or take to church or give at a funeral home.

Red Rose Bush
Photo by author 2005

So, as we became closer on our drive to Byers (Bergoo) or #4 as the mining town was called, I could only see piles of coal everywhere. No homes where I remembered them. I had to slowly open and close my eyes to remember how things had looked when I lived here. When I finally thought I had found where my old house stood, something red was sticking out of a pile of coal. That pile of coal must have been a hundred feet high, it seemed and I didn't care as I jumped out of the car, kicking off my shoes. And in my nice white pants, I started crawling up that old pile of coal. I had found a red rose...my red rose. It was surely from my mother's old rose bushes and I remember it had a dirty black root. I carefully wrapped it and brought it back to Ohio where we lived. I planted it and today (2012) I am cutting red roses from my childhood.

The highway rolls alongside old railroad tracks at Bergoo
Photo by author 2016

The old trestle bridge my mom used to walk on as a child
Photo by author 2016

My mom touched so many lives, both those of family and strangers because she never met one. She had many stories from her childhood in Webster County and she shared them with family and friends. Although she told us she often felt trapped by the mountains and wondered what was on the other side of them, she was proud to be from West Virginia, as I am. I have lived in the state of my mother's birth for ten years now. Every time I travel the old windy road through Bergoo, you can bet I look for those red roses. One day I hope to cut my own.

CHAPTER 16

THE PRINGLE BROTHERS

Sycamore trees. We know them for their unusual looking bark and as one of the oldest species of trees on Earth. These trees also have a long history in folklore dating back thousands of years to the Egyptian times. Many Egyptians believed the Holy Sycamore connected the worlds between the dead and the living. Native American Indians called them the *Ghosts of the Forest* and two brothers in Upshur County lived in a large one for over three years. Can you even imagine? If this were a TV series, it would be called *Tiny House Living Frontier Style.*

The Pringle brothers, Samuel and John, deserted the army at Fort Pitt back in 1761 as this was during the French and Indian Wars. They hailed from the South Branch Valley area of the Potomac River and served in the British Garrison where

Pittsburgh, Pennsylvania is located today. Apparently unhappy with the hard life and servitude of a soldier, they left without permission and ventured into the backwoods. The Pringle boys decided to prevent possible detection by going deeper into the forest and followed the Tygart River Valley until they reached the Buckhannon River, near what is now Buckhannon, West Virginia. There they made their home in a giant, hollow sycamore tree that they had discovered. The tree was nearly eleven feet in diameter and would suffice nicely as temporary housing. As legend has it, *temporary* lasted for several years! They cleared out leaves and debris that cluttered up the inside, made a fireplace inside the tree with rocks from the river and used a large knothole up high in the tree as a smoke vent for their small fires. It was cozy by any frontier standards and served its purpose....a hideout from all who would possibly find them as deserters, which could end in death for them both.

Historical signage at the tree
Photo by author

The Pringle Tree as it stood in 2015
Photo by author

A few years passed and John decided to head back to the South Branch Valley area in 1867 as ammunition and supplies were beginning to thin out. Leaving the last two charges of ammo with his brother, John set out on his adventure to the valley and left Samuel to fend for himself. Legend says that during his brother's absence, Samuel suffered mentally and physically as he was greatly worried about his brother's welfare and if he would return. In later weeks, his provisions were nearly exhausted and he was barely alive when his brother arrived back home. John took seven weeks on his adventure and when he returned to the tree he carried unexpected good news...the war had ended and they could possibly go home! The brothers surely discussed the pros and cons of leaving their snug home and eventually decided that they would take their chances on returning to civilization---even with the possibility of being killed for desertion.

The author at the Pringle Tree 2013

The brothers eventually left their tree home and rejoined society. The next year, Samuel ended his bachelor days, married Charity Cutright, and settled down as a happily married man. In 1769, the brothers led a small group of settlers back to the Buckhannon Valley to begin a permanent settlement there.

And what of the great sycamore tree? A descendant of the tree still stands at the mouth of Tukey Run where John and Samuel lived for over three years. The current tree is mammoth by modest standards but is not as grand as the original as this one is the third generation sprung from the roots of the famous tree. A highway historic marker on U.S. 119 north of Buckhannon marks the legendary location. Feel like a road trip to see this famous tree? The Pringle Tree Park is open to the public from May 1 to November 1 and is maintained by the Upshur County Commission.

CHAPTER 17

Law and Order Comes to Booger Hole

A fter dusting off some old newspapers at my dad's house, I came across an old tattered column bragging how the *Law* had wiped out the little community of Booger Hole of its unruly characters and outlaws. One of my columns I wrote for Two Lane Livin' publication a few years ago featured a ghostly tale from this area of Big Otter Creek. I felt obliged to share with you another side of the coin now, the human side.

In the early 1900s, around a dozen mysterious murders and more disappearances occurred during a time span of a little more than a year. The exact numbers and names of those who died are unknown as many of the disappearances went unreported due to widespread fear of retribution in the community.

In a 1917 newspaper article, Booger Hole was mentioned as a violent area where thieves, murderers and unsolved crimes were the norm. Keep in mind these were the post-Civil War days when men feared their neighbors and suspicions of rebels and unionists could cost you your life. As late as 1918, law-abiding citizens tired of the area's riff raff and lawlessness and took matters into their own hands. A handbill was passed around and posted in various areas stating the seriousness of the situation. It is shared here in the exact style it was written. It reads:

WE, THE CITIZENS OF CLAY COUNTY,

SEEING THAT WE CANNOT GET JUSTICE BY LAW

HAVE ORGANIZED THE CLAY COUNTY MOB.

WE HAVE PLEDGED OUR LIVES TO DRIVE THESE PEOPLE FROM OUR COUNTY OR KILL THEM.

IF WE CANNOT CATCH AND HANG YOU, WE WILL SNEAK UPON AND KILL YOU AS YOU KILLED HENRY HARGIS, LACY ANN BOGGS, THE OLD PEDDLER AND PRESTON TANNER.

IF BEFORE YOU LEAVE, THERE IS ANY STEALING, KILLING OR BURNING, WE WILL GET THE BLOOD HOUNDS AND DETECTIVES AND RUN YOU TO THE ENDS OF THE EARTH.

NILL SAMPSON, KOOCH SAMPSON, FRED MOORE AND AARON RUNYON ARE HEREBY NOTIFIED TO LEAVE THE STATE IN TEN DAYS.

ROSE LYONS, BILL MOORE AND ELIZABETH SAMPSON ARE NOTIFIED TO LEAVE IN THIRTY DAYS.

PS DO NOT STOP THIS SIDE OF THE OHIO RIVER.

Booger Hole Building
Photo by the author 2010

The people of Clay County were fed up. They had enough of the lawlessness, violence and chaos. To many folks, the senseless killing of Lacy Ann Boggs was the final straw. Lucy was an elderly lady who knew a great deal of the goings on around the holler, but she was smart enough to keep her mouth closed. Unfortunately, this was not the case when several men questioned her about the missing body of one Henry "Ben" Hargis. Old Lucy was said to touch her lamplighter to her pipe and with a grin said, "Why I know exactly where he is." The very next day she was found dead, shot to death in her favorite chair with her beloved pipe on her lap. Apparently, some folks did not want his body discovered and found a way to keep the old lady silent - forever.

Murder occurred often in this hideaway of a place among the mountains. In an old newspaper clipping, violence was apparent when Preston Tanner had his head bashed in by a claw hammer after a night of card playing with twenty-one-year old Howard Sampson.

1971 Charleston Daily Mail Newspaper Clipping

One of the first mysterious deaths to occur in Booger Hole happened around 1893, when Henry Hargis, along with a cool three hundred dollars he was carrying, went missing. Several residents of the hollow were accused of murdering him, but all had alibis, and no conviction was made.

Odd and eccentric characters dotted the landscape of Booger Hole. James Moore would go into spells of shouting and screaming, gazing at the ground as if something was about to rise from the soil. (Some thought Moore may have killed Henry Hargess.)

People disappeared from Booger Hole and many were never found. Joseph Clark, a watchmaker who stopped to sleep overnight in the Booger Hole schoolhouse, was another victim to disappear in the area. His body was never found, but a trail of blood led officers to a nearby creek. The case was never solved.

Dirt Road Near Booger Hole 2010
Photo by author

In 1902 John Newman, a Swedish peddler, rode into Booger Hole to peddle his wares. He disappeared and was never seen again. Traces of blood believed to be from the peddler's body were found in a barn, but the suspect killed a young colt to cover up the evidence, as blood was everywhere. The prosecutor disguised himself in prisoner's clothing, complete with ball and chain, and went undercover in the jail. He won the confidence of the suspect, and was told all the horrible details of the immigrant peddler's murder. When this evidence was presented in the trial, however, the judge ruled entrapment and threw out the evidence and the state's case. The accused killer was not convicted, and he returned to Booger Hole.

Charleston Mail Newspaper 1917

Eventually the law and the righteous law abiding folk won out. Court cases were won slowly, one at a time, many arrests were made and the outlaws and lowlifes figured out that they best be moving out of Booger Hole and finding a new place to haunt. Booger Holes reputation healed after a few decades and everyone began to rest a bit easier among the living. Now the dead??? Well, I will save that story for another time.

CHAPTER 18

Murder Box in the Courthouse Attic

I t was a hot muggy summer day and we had managed to climb
the staircase in the old courthouse that led to the attic without
having a heart attack. Under a pitched roof and in the
sweltering humidity of a windowless attic room, we sat down and
began to examine the old dusty covered books and yellowing
documents. My cousin and I had travelled to a distant county in
West Virginia to research our family line. This somewhat elusive
sixth great grandfather settled in the tiny community of Brake.
Armed with some notebooks, cameras and pencils we began our
courthouse search for some information on our family.

Old Post Card of Hardy County Courthouse

We found actual deeds, marriage records and death records dating back to the early 1800's. Some were yellowed and crumbling and a few were eaten along the edges by an apparent rodent infestation. It was growing hotter by the minute and after what seemed like an eternity, I stood up from our little table to stretch. As I pulled my chair back, my foot hit something solid under the table. I crouched down to look and after seeing the medium sized cardboard box, I pulled it out from its hiding spot and shook it. My cousin looked at me and nodded and I shook the unmarked box again to test its contents. Something heavy tipped the box on its side and I have to admit that my curiosity got the best of me. Reaching down inside, I lifted up the top ingredients which were a series of glossy 8x10 black and white photographs. I was not sure what I was expecting to see...but murder scene photographs were not on my top five list. As we looked at the photos one by one, we became a voyeur into someone's nightmare. It seemed that the victim had surely died on scene as we flipped thru the glossy prints. Blood spatters on an old wallpapered wall in someone's kitchen took center stage in the first photos. Large amounts of blood on the walls and linoleum had caused puddles, which looked surprisingly eerie in black and white. Judging from the setting and the antiquated kitchen appliances, this crime had taken place in the 1940's. The next few photos took our discovery to another level. The lifeless body was face down in the next photo. The man's lifeless arms were extended to the side of the body as if he were hugging the old kitchen floor. The last photo showed a blood covered axe with a short handle located just a few feet from the body.

Murder Box in the Attic
Photo by author

We laid the murder scene photos on our genealogy pile that was strewn across the table and I reached down into the box and picked up the next and final item. It was wrapped in a brown paper bag and was a bit heavy so I promptly handed it to my cousin telling him it was his turn for discovery. As he unwrapped the item slowly, I think we could almost have guessed what it was. The handle was a short beat up piece of light colored wood covered in what looked like rust. Well, at least we thought it was rust but after seeing it was the same axe in the photos, we knew it was dried blood. We gawked at it for a few minutes and wondered how a murder tool and the crime scene photos ended up in the courthouse attic. We had lost our appetite for discovery that afternoon and the 110 degree attic wasn't helping any either. We put our genealogy files away, returned the deed books and other items to their places of rest and ceremoniously wrapped up the photos and axe sticking them back into their cardboard home. We silently left not mentioning what we had found to any staff in the offices below.

Many years have passed since that hot summer day in Hardy County and my cousin and I have only mentioned the murder box once to each other since then. I often wonder if it is still there and I plan to explore that attic room when I am in the area again. I'd like to find out more…wouldn't you?

CHAPTER 19

Halloween Haunts and an Old Tavern

Being a paranormal researcher for over twenty five years has put me in many a haunted building. I always jump at the chance to investigate a new place and love digging up the dark history associated with it. I hardly ever think twice about a chance to investigate...except for that one time back in 1988. Now THAT my friend, was a totally unexpected visit from a ghost.

I had traveled to central West Virginia to join up with some of my friends to go camping for the weekend. My friends were locals in that little town and had lived there all of their lives. I was excited to visit there again and so close to Halloween! We had all driven separate that night and had agreed to meet up at this little hole in the wall tavern. Darkness and stale cigarette smoke met me head on and as I blinked repeatedly, my vision gradually adjusted to the shadows inside. The entire bar had been transformed into a weird cemetery scene. Since Halloween was the very next night, I considered it appropriate but a bit odd. There were fake Styrofoam headstones propped up across a small area I imagined was used for dancing. The pool table was draped in black crepe paper and little white ghosts dangled from the ceiling by bits and pieces of fishing line. The bartender was dressed up like a saloon girl and some of the patrons were dressed in an odd assortment of put together costumes. My friends were nowhere to be seen but as usual, I was early and they tended to be late. I grabbed a barstool and ordered up a beer. I got the typical "You aren't from around here" questions and as I learned everyone's name at the bar. I soon noticed a solo man sitting back in the corner of the room behind me. His legs were crossed out in front of him, he was leaning back on two legs of the chair and I could tell he was very tall, even as he sat. He was dressed as a coal miner complete with black soot or coal dust rubbed across his face making his eyes stand out in the shadows. He nodded and I nodded back. Turning back to the patrons sitting at the bar I immediately was drawn back into their conversation. I forgot about the man when my two buddies arrived and we sat for another hour or so talking with the bartender and swapping stories.

The bartender laughed and then got a serious look on her face as she told me that the bar was *truly* a haunted place. I said sure, everywhere is haunted as I laughed not believing her. She told me about the old mine whose entrance was just across the road. Apparently, that tavern we were sitting in had been there since the early 1930's and the day of the mine explosion, the place had been turned into a triage area. Injured miners were laid across the long bar and on the tables awaiting medical help, as the area was so remote it took ambulances over an hour to arrive. Several died while waiting and one of those souls apparently visited the bar in spirit form. The day of the accident, he was put in the corner and laid across a big table. The bartender told me he was so tall his limbs hung over the wooden table nearly touching the floor and it was there....on that table in the corner where he had died. He is still here, she told us. People see him stalking around that area, sitting at the table and he even spooked the help on occasion, she said. I already knew the answer to my question but I went ahead and asked. She pointed directly behind me to the corner I had seen that man sitting in. When I saw his miners clothing earlier, I had figured it was another bar patron dressed for Halloween. I turned slowly, half expecting to see him still sitting there and of course, his chair was empty. My friends and I left the bar, talked briefly outside and then got in our separate cars and drove off. I looked in my rear view mirror more than a few times that night half expecting to see a miner sitting behind me. I never went back into that bar again as it burned down years later. I wonder if he haunts that stretch of remote road or if he finally found peace. I am hoping he's at peace.

CHAPTER 20

Oh, Death

"The character of a community is revealed by the way it honors its loved ones"

The family cemetery in Appalachia has played an important role in social life, local history, and culture since frontiersmen arrived such as Daniel Boone, Morgan Morgan, Jesse Hughes and Lewis Wetzel. These early settlers and pioneers were coming into a country in which there were no roads, no established towns and no prior history by their own kind of people. It was a rugged and dangerous environment. In a very short time, death from childbirth, accidents, Indian warfare, and communicable diseases began to take their toll.

Meadowland Cemetery, Bergoo, West Virginia
Photo by the author 2010

Our brave settlers would found a piece of land they intended to call home and then they would bury their dead on this property. This would typically be chosen at the time the need first arose. For example, the first grave would be dug and that spot would be designated the family cemetery for the Gregory's, the Dodrill's, the Hamrick's or the Miller's. These first burials were usually located on a piece of high ground, frequently with a good view of the surrounding area. It was often a beloved spot of the head of the household. There was also a common belief that on resurrection morning, the dead in Christ would arise with the first rays of the morning sun. The higher elevations usually got morning sunshine earlier than low-lying ground. It was also common for graves to be placed with the face of the dead toward the sunrise in the east-west orientation so commonly found in old Christian burials.

Small Family Cemetery up the Back Fork of Elk River
Near Webster Springs
Photo by the author 2016

Death became an important part of Appalachian culture because it was so commonplace, so ever present and looming. It touched every person without regard to race, religion, age or status quo. The living dealt with whatever life handed them. Many times, it made them stronger. I remember the old saying "If it doesn't kill you, it'll make you stronger". Mountain folk commemorated death, they respected it and they even sang songs about it.

The typical family cemeteries of long ago have been replaced by larger community cemeteries. Many fieldstones carved and placed at loved ones graves have toppled, been reclaimed by the earth or become illegible in their writings. Names, dates and heartfelt messages left on stones have borne the brunt of the elements and the passing of time. Many are lost forever. These pioneering souls, these trail blazers of the past were the sturdy, mountain stock that many of us can claim as ancestors.

Richwood, West Virginia Cemetery
Photo by author 2015

Riverview Cemetery in Parkersburg, West Virginia
Photo by the author 2009

These were the early settlers and pioneers who planted crops, built cabins, taught school, inspired us to worship and made the community strong. These cemeteries are not only a symbol of the past, but a connection to our future as the descendants of these families. Cemeteries can reveal information about historic events, religions, lifestyles, and genealogy. Let us not forget them.

CHAPTER 21

Mountains, Holly & Mistletoe

C hristmas in the mountains of West Virginia! What could be more perfect than a warm fire in the stove, a Christmas tree in the corner, a wreath of holly above the mantle and a sprig of mistletoe above the doorway? Did you know that holly and mistletoe have pagan originations?

In Roman mythology, holly was the sacred plant of the god Saturn, and to honor him at the Saturnalia festival, the Romans gave each other gifts of holly wreaths. When Christians began to celebrate the birth of Jesus, they risked being persecuted for their new religion, and to avoid detection, they would place holly wreaths in their houses. As far as passerby were concerned, they were celebrating Saturnalia, not Christmas.

Holly on the hillside
Photo by author 2010

Gradually, Christian popularity increased, their customs became commonplace, and holly lost its links to Paganism and became a traditional symbol of Christmas. Over the many centuries, holly has become a symbol for peace and joy, and people often settled disputes under a holly tree.

In Germany, a sprig of holly that was used in church decorations is believed to protect homes from lightning strikes, and in England farmers decorated their beehives with holly because they believed that at the first Christmas bees hummed in honor of the baby Jesus. These beliefs all contributed towards *decking the halls with boughs* of holly being popular at Christmas.

The Norseman, the ancient Celts and the Native Americans Indians revered mistletoe as a sacred plant. The Druids believed that mistletoe could protect against thunderstorms and lightning strikes. Priests would use a golden sickle to cut a piece of mistletoe from a revered oak tree, catching the branches before they reached the ground. The mistletoe would then be cut into small pieces and distributed among the local people.

Mistletoe Branch

Olde Woodcut of an Ancient Druid
Origin unknown

Mistletoe was also a recognized as a druidic symbol of joy and peace. If enemies met each other underneath the woodland mistletoe, they were obliged to put down their weapons and form a truce until the following day. This is where the custom of hanging a sprig ball of mistletoe from the ceiling and kissing under it originates.

Whatever your religion or beliefs at this special time of year, I hope you can find peace, love and make many memories while celebrating Christmas with loved ones. Be sure to light a candle to remember your loved ones on the other side, as well.

CHAPTER 22

HATFIELD CEMETERY

I had ventured into a remote southern part of the state, the area where my husband always told me not to go alone. What? Don't go there alone? I was an adult. I had a gun for extreme protection, pepper spray for anything ornery and a pretty good intuition that got me out of trouble a few times in my life. Plus, I had maps and a cell phone. What could happen, I thought?

The day started out easy enough with beautiful weather for a drive on that late summer afternoon. I had filled up the vehicle with gas and made sure I had a notebook and camera as I planned on getting some good photographs along the drive. Where was I headed? I was adventuring into Hatfield-McCoy territory intent on getting some good cemetery and scenery shots.

Hatfield Marker Sign
Photo by author 2012

Travel was quick that day and I arrived in early in the afternoon. I had done some research on the fighting clans a few years prior but was really excited about boots on the ground and a chance to explore on my own. If you are not familiar with the tragic tale, this historic event involved two rural families of the West Virginia–Kentucky area along the Tug Fork of the Big Sandy River. The family feud lasted from 1863 until about 1891. The dark history of these families was violent and resulted in many deaths, threats of harm and imprisonments. However, the event that launched the now-infamous conflict—which claimed the lives of 13 family members—has taken a backseat to the fact of its impressive longevity. What caused the bad blood in the first place? It started because of a hog. Relations between the two families soured over a seemingly small matter: a dispute over a single hog. More about that in a minute. The Hatfield's were more affluent than the McCoy's and were well connected politically.

Devil Anse Hatfield
Public Domain /Wikimedia Commons Credit

A couple of court decisions helped to fuel this all-consuming feud. In the late 1870s, Devil Anse Hatfield got into a land dispute with McCoy's cousin, attorney Perry Cline. Hatfield won the land dispute and was granted Cline's entire five thousand acres of land. A few months after the verdict, Randolph McCoy stopped to visit Floyd Hatfield, a cousin of Devil Anse. While visiting, McCoy saw a hog that he said had the McCoy marking on its ear. Hatfield denied the accusation and the two were hauled into court with Preacher and Justice of the Peace, Anderson Hatfield to settle the suit. Both Hatfields and McCoys served as jurors. Randolph's nephew Bill Staton, also a brother-in-law of Ellison Hatfield, swore that Floyd Hatfield owned the hog. Floyd won the case. To add to the heated matter, Staton was killed in a shootout in June of 1880 with Paris and Sam McCoy, who were sent to prison for their crime.

Photograph is public domain and dated 1897
Wikimedia Commons Credit

Top row, from left to right: Rosa Lee Hatfield (daughter of Anderson), Detroit 'Troy' Hatfield (son of Anderson), Betty Hatfield (Caldwell) (daughter of Anderson), Elias Hatfield (son of

Anderson), Tom Chafin (nephew of William Anderson), Joe D. Hatfield (son of William Anderson), Ock Damron, Shephard Hatfield (son of Cap), Levicy Emma Hatfield (daughter of Cap), and Bill Border (store clerk).

Second row, from left to right: Mrs. Mary Hensley-Simpkins-Howes (daughter of Anderson) with daughter Vici Simpkins, William Anderson 'Devil Anse' Hatfield, Levicy Chafin Hatfield (wife of Anderson), Nancy Elizabeth Hatfield (wife of Cap) with son Robert Elliott Hatfield, Louise Hatfield (daughter of Cap), Cap Hatfield, and Coleman Hatfield (son of Cap)

Front row, from left to right: Tennyson 'Tennis' Hatfield (son of Anderson), Levicy Hatfield (daughter of Johnse), Willis Hatfield (son of Anderson), and 'Watch' or 'Yellow Watch' ('Devil Anse's' coon and bear dog)

To add a Romeo and Juliet taste to the tale was the short-lived romance between Johnse Hatfield and Roseanna McCoy in 1880. After she became pregnant, Roseanna moved in with the Hatfields, which of course infuriated her family. Several months into her pregnancy, Johnse decided to flirt (and marry) another McCoy. Nancy was Roseanna's cousin and apparently married Johnse out of immature revenge directed to Roseanna. To make matters worse, Roseanna and Johnse's little daughter died of the measles when she was just eight months old.

The Hatfield-McCoy saga captivated me at a young age. I was already learning about Jesse James, Al Capone, Wild Bill Hickok and Butch Cassidy and the Sundance Kid, when I was in 6th grade. It wasn't long before I was reading every book I could find on this Appalachian feud.

Captain Anderson and Levicy Marker
Photo by author 2012

My adventure took an exciting turn as I found the road for the Hatfield Cemetery. I had been there once before, many years ago and my memory was second-guessing the last turn...but...I found it! The graveyard is located near Sarah Ann, in Logan County, West Virginia. The earliest known burial dates back to 1898 and is the grave of Captain S. Hatfield. This mountain cemetery features the grave and monument with a life-size statue of Captain Anderson "Devil Anse" Hatfield, which was erected in 1926.

I gathered my camera, notebook and pepper spray (just in case) and headed into the burial ground to read graves, leave some flowers and pay my respects.

Hatfield Cemetery approach
Photo by author 2012

The large statue of Devil Anse commands your attention. He was quite a character, it seems. Born in what is today Logan County, West Virginia, he grew up in the hill country along the Tug Fork River and developed a formidable reputation as a talented marksman and equestrian. With his wife, Levicy, he produced nine boys and four girls, owned considerable land and ran a successful lumbering operation. A Confederate sympathizer after the start of the Civil War, he formed the Logan Wildcat's band after West Virginia became a state by declaration of President Lincoln and was admitted to the Union in 1863. What a colorful, exciting albeit tragic life he led. He spent the last years of his life quietly on his farm and converted to Christianity in 1911. After a lifetime of being agnostic, he was baptized in the river at the age of seventy-three. Although violence followed him everywhere, he was never wounded. Devil Anse succumbed to pneumonia ten years after his immersion by water into faith. His funeral was (at that time) the largest ever held in Logan County.

Old newspaper cover depicting the head of families
Williamson Daily News

Wandering around the perimeter of the cemetery, a small bouquet of flowers got my attention. They were simple wildflowers tied with a piece of brown twine but lie randomly placed as if tossed quickly onto the dirt path. The grave closest to the flowers was about five feet away. The flowers were still fresh as if someone, just minutes earlier, had picked them. I bent over, picked the flowers up and as I smelled them, I turned towards the largest statue, Devil Anse. A butterfly twirled around the statue and as I watched it (I have a thing for butterflies!) there was the sound of footsteps on gravel behind me. Let me remind you, access to this cemetery is a bit tricky, you just don't turn off the main road and drive up here. You have to hike it basically, so when I heard the sound of footsteps, I patted my pocket of pepper spray as I turned to see who was there. This is where my day took an odd turn. My gaze was greeted with thin air. No body stood where there *should* be a body standing.

Hatfield Cemetery
Photo by author 2012

Graveyards are serene places gathering people to think, reflect and mourn those who have passed on. On that summer day though, it was anything but serene. The air around me turned chilly and I had the distinct feeling that I was not alone. Everyone knows that strange feeling, the hair stands up on the back of your neck and you realize that there are eyes upon you that you cannot see. Something in my psyche told me to return the flowers to where I had found them. I walked over to the path, laid them where I had found them and decided to call it a day. I wandered around the cemetery admiring the large statue of Devil Anse, took some photographs, read some burial names and dates and prepared to hike back to my vehicle.

It takes a lot to unsettle my nerves. I visit haunted and paranormal active locations all the time. For nearly thirty years I have researched and investigated the paranormal so for me to be a bit *unsettled* is a new feeling for me. Once or twice, on my hike back to the vehicle I could swear I heard footsteps behind me so when I was finally in the car, I relaxed a bit and reviewed some of my photographs that I had just taken. In one photo of the cemetery, an unusual mist was evident in the background. It was a perfect weather day so I was a bit puzzled as to what I had captured. It wasn't foggy, it wasn't rainy or misty and no one was smoking of course, I was the only human there. What was in my photo? Who knows? My excitement grew with the prospects of capturing something paranormal. When I returned to the office that evening, I excitedly downloaded my photos from my camera. Eleven were missing. You guessed it. A whole series of photos, including my mist photo, were missing from my camera. I was crushed. Until this very day, when I hear mention of the Hatfield-McCoys or think of that day, I remember that bouquet of fresh wild flowers and that unusual graveyard mist and I shiver. I cannot wait to go back. For such an area fraught with feuds, murder and death, it still felt serene.

And what about the blood battle? Between 1880 and 1891, the feud claimed more than a dozen members of the two families. On one occasion, the governors of West Virginia and Kentucky even threatened to have their militias invade each other's states. As the feud came to an end in 1891, the stories all faded a bit. Both family leaders attempted to withdraw into relative oblivion and live in peace. Randolph McCoy, Devil Anse's enemy and foe, became a local ferry operator. In 1914, he died at the age of eight-eight from burns suffered in an accidental fire. By all accounts, it was said he continued to be haunted by the deaths of his children and rightly so as they all paid a deadly price. Even though "Devil" Anse Hatfield, who had long proclaimed his skepticism about religion, was born again later in life, I wonder if his faith wavered? Although the conflict subsided generations ago, the names Hatfield and McCoy continue to loom large in the American imagination.

CHAPTER 23

WHIPPLE BLACK MIST

One of my favorite locations to investigate since discovering it in 2009, is the old coal company store in Fayette County, West Virginia. Whipple Company store was built in 1890 with a gigantic 18,000 square foot imprint. The Whipple Company Store in the coal-mining glory days provided just about everything and anything the coal miner and his family would need. Entire families lived in the coal camp with the men and older boys working at the mine. Although the Company Store had its benefits to the coal miner and their families, it did not go without reputation. The coal companies owned the store, the newspaper, the homes, the goods, the miner, and their money. Whipple Company Store was designed by the Coal Baron, Justus Collins. Justus was man of merit and great means. This coal company store is one of four that he had built. Today the only one left standing is this white beauty at the junction of County Roads 15 and 21/20 in Scarbro, right off of US Route 19.

Photo credit to Whipple Coal Company Store

Inside the store, its employees could use scrip (company-specific legal tender) in which workers were paid for goods like food, equipment, grains, meat, clothing and shoes.   Basically, anything could be purchased in the company store from candy to caskets. The building's octagonal shape was designed as a way to control the workers, for the store's one employee could stand dead center in the store on the ground floor and the room itself became an echo chamber, providing the company managers with all the intelligence it needed to maintain the upper hand over its workers.

Outside of Whipple Store
Photo by author 2016

Over the years of investigating this property, we grew to love its history, albeit dark history and uniqueness. We wanted to offer it to people as a location to explore for its paranormal activity and the history so we decided to offer our Ghost Hunting 101 Class as an event.

First floor general store area during Ghost Hunting 101 class
with the author.
Photo by Perry Queener 2011

Ghost Hunting 101 classes are a scheduled event in which people meet us at a location to learn the history and hauntings and then at the conclusion of class, they get the opportunity to explore and investigate the premises. At Whipple Coal Company Store, this was a true privilege to schedule and facilitate. Our class was set for a May evening in 2011 and my husband, Perry was present to help. Perry was a person of great interest and help at our events at the Whipple Store as he is a mining engineer and very familiar with coal mining means and equipment. He has been in all kinds of mines from deep mines, drift, slope and worked on many strip jobs, of course. He helped us identify various coal mining equipment in the museum and told us of some of his experiences working in mines.

The class went well that night. There were thirty souls in attendance with many of these folks including people I met through my prior ghost hunting adventures. A few were new to the field and were very excited as this was their first time investigating. The class itself lasted about two hours and we covered a brief history of the company store, the local coal camp town and Perry showed a few mining tools and implements to the group. As participants were seated in the General Store area and I was speaking, I remember pausing and looking around as people seemed to be murmuring amongst themselves. The unmistakable scent of pipe smoke wafted among us. I remember asking if anyone smelled anything unusual to which several nodded in agreement. Windows were closed in the building and no one was smoking of course. We all were slightly excited to have experienced the phenomena and more surprised when the owner of the building pointed out the store manager's office was connected to the area where we were holding our class. Surely, back in the day, the manager and staff of the store would have smoked pipes or cigars? This phenomenon had been experienced prior to our visit on several occasions by other visitors, we were told. How cool is that?

We did a quick walk around tour of the levels and rooms we had access to. The lower level basement, the first floor store area housed a small granary room, a freight room, a restroom, offices and a post office, a vault and a switchboard. The top floor included a once popular ballroom with faded golden yellow paint and several small rooms. The freight elevator and a staircase connected the levels with the elevator being a true treasure as it was hand operated. After a quick walk around tour, we turned everyone loose to explore on their own. Perry and I wandered around exploring as well and we soon separated. It was halfway thru the evening that he and I met back up in the freight room by the basement door. He told me he felt "funny" and that I should be taking a lot of photos.

Signage outside of the Whipple Store
Photo by author 2011

My husband tends to have a "sense" about him at times so I listened to him, grabbed my camera and began taking photos as he walked in that room. The following is a series of photos that I took. In the first one, you can see my husband standing looking at me. He had just said you had better start taking some photos, as it feels "funky" in here. You see my husband in the photo below. This is right after he told me to take some photos. You can make out a darker shadow area to the left of his head.

Photo by the author 2011

Photo by the author 2011

As the freight room cleared out, I took some more photographs and in each one an unusual shadow appeared. This was with a digital camera so the flash is built into the body of the camera itself.

So what exactly did we capture? I will leave that up to you.

Here are some things we can rule out:
- It wasn't cigarette or vape smoke. No smoking allowed on our investigations or inside of the Whipple Store.
- It is not a human shadow. Perry and I were the only two in the room when I took the last two photos
- It is not a camera strap or a shadow of one hanging by the camera. I had none.
- It is not a finger. I am very careful with the placement of my hands and fingers when snapping photographs.
- It is not human hair hanging in front of the camera.

The old hand operated elevator shaft on the first floor
Photo by author 2011

We are left with no concrete conclusion and an anomaly. You could say it is paranormal because *paranormal* means it is not typical and not scientifically explainable. The room that we were in (the freight room) has seen violence in the past with a shooting. It is also in the area where the old elevator can be accessed. A man was found dead hanging in the elevator shaft many years ago. This room also is the access to the grain room where bags of grains could be purchased and filled. An unfortunate man many years ago was found dead with his head shoved into a bag of grain. Could it be the energy of these poor souls?

As of the writing of this book in 2019, the old Whipple Coal Company Store is ready for a new chapter. The owners have sold it in the fall of 2018 and the new owner has taken possession of this historic building. It will be interesting to see what is next for the spirits of Whipple.

CHAPTER 24

SITTIN' UP WITH THE DEAD

My Mother was born in a small coal mining community in Webster County, West Virginia. Bergoo was a remote community but what it lacked in convenience it made up for in beauty as it was surrounded by mountains and expansive forestland. One of the local coalmines was called #4 and was owned by the Pardee and Curtin Company. Many were employed at the mines, including my grandfather, Otley Green.

Everyone knew each other and many houses were related by blood. Due to the remoteness of the area families tended to stay put and marry other local families leading to hundreds of cousins and descendants of many of the same pioneer for many of us.

People helped each other out in times of need whether it was for food, employment, the birthing of a child or the celebration of a marriage. It's hard to imagine, in the mobile, disposable society we now live in, that this kind of concern for your neighbors was something upon which you could rely, but it was. My mother often spoke of the generosity of neighbors in the form of groceries dropped off and much needed medicine being made available.

The author's mother, Suzi (far right) in Bergoo with her sisters
Dixie, Nan and Lou in the 1950's.
Photo from the family collection

Bergoo area near # 4 Mine
Photo by author 2016

Death also brought people together. The local funeral home was about a forty-five minute drive away and many did not have transportation. Death was taken care at the home and by the families. Graves would often be dug my hand and by someone who knew the deceased. There was a more personal touch to the passing of one's body back in those days. In decades past, many smaller rural communities had no access to a mortuary or funeral home. The tasks of preparing the body for burial and constructing the casket were done not by a mortician, but the community members themselves.

Typical 19th century home viewing
Wikimedia Commons/Public Domain image

The practice of watching over a body springs from the oldest religious traditions. Scholars say the ancient Romans took the custom with them as they conquered the Mediterranean and Europe. By the Middle Ages, the practice was wrapped into Christianity and came with the first European settlers to the New World. There were often prayers, hymns and lit candles at the head and the feet of the body. However, with the rise of funeral homes in the early 20th century, the home-based wake declined and evolved into "visitations" or viewings at funeral parlors.

A young nun digging a grave while another nun looks on.
Painting by John Everett Millais.
Wikimedia Commons/Public Domain image

My mother often told us tales of her and her family sitting up with the dead. Mom said it was done out of respect, of course, but also out of necessity. The body would be washed, dressed and then laid out in the parlor or suitable room of choosing. This room would typically be a front room or a room with a large doorway to allow passage of the casket. My mom would also tell us that someone would volunteer to sit up with the body overnight. Mom would chuckle and mention someone had to keep the cats out of the room and I remember as a child, I was always too afraid to ask why. Other customs she mentioned to me was the placing of coins on the deceased eyes to help the lids remain closed. Pennies

Sherri Brake

would not be used because they could turn the skin green so often it was the use of nickels or quarters. In my years of researching death and funeral customs, I came to find out that this custom dates back to the ancient Greeks and payment for the Ferryman to aid in crossing the River Styx or River Acheron, the waterway in the depths of the Greek Underworld.

A sycamore coffin contains a mummified body
of an Egyptian woman.
Wikimedia Commons /Public Domain

Every civilization has its own distinct way of life, it also has its own way of death and burying. The dead, after all, have to be disposed of by the living and funerary practices are deeply embedded in society and culture. When a man or woman dies, the daughters and sons survive and though death comes daily here on Earth, such are the cycles by which a society endures. In the Jewish faith, one of their mourning traditions is to *sit shiva* at the home of the deceased (or principal mourner) for seven days. The word *shiva* means seven in Hebrew. Family and friends visit to pay their respects.

120

In Ireland, the traditional Catholic wake is still carried out. Soon after the death, word of mouth will spread the news and neighbors will help in preparing food and drinks and alcoholic beverages. The corpse will normally be dressed in white linen and laid out in their own bed. Candles are usually lit and the corpse is never left alone. The "Irish Wake" was a traditional mourning custom practiced in Ireland until the mid-1970s. The customs are now only practiced in full in remote Irish towns that honor tradition.

One of the most studied civilizations placed the ritual of death at the very heart of public life. The Egyptians celebrated with death masks, mummies and grand tombs for their royalty. The afterlife, or *Duat,* was believed to be much like the land of the living. Preparation for the journey was ever important and could involve burial of a servant, pet dog and other creature comforts for the afterlife such as ornate furniture and supplies of food.

Ancient cemetery in Greece
Photo Wikimedia Commons/Public Domain

In funerary practices, as in so much else, the Romans followed the lead of the Greeks. The conception of the afterlife was much the same. So too were their burial rites, but they seem to have felt more strongly than the Greeks that death was something to be kept at a distance. The Roman dead were banished in areas away from the living with cemeteries being established outside of the city limits. Often tombs and cemeteries were established on main roads arriving and departing from a major city.

On the subject of burials, I have been told that on some occasions, lumber had been put away for the purpose of constructing a casket. In Appalachia, a very fine casket could be made from cherry lumber and if that kind of wood was used, the deceased person was a little bit better off financially than most folks were. Most of the time, it was pine or poplar that a casket was made from. Food was brought to the home of the deceased person by neighbors, and those who came to sit up were always invited to partake of what had been brought in. The graves were all hand-dug, using picks and shovels. Again, this was usually done by neighbors. This task was especially hard during the cold winter months.

Prior to having air conditioning, decorative veils were occasionally draped over the casket. These were most often used in hot weather when the deceased person's body was kept at home prior to the funeral service. Veils were useful in keeping annoying flies away. During summer months when windows and door were kept open for air to circulate, someone with a fly swat would sometimes stand near the casket and make use of the fly swatter as they occasional also shooed the cat away. I think it would make for a dreadfully long night.

I often think of those odd conversations with my mother about death out in the country and the keeping away of cats from the viewing room. Seems as those these days we view death from a greater distance and at funeral homes that are cold and impersonal. Yes, many of us fear the "Great Equalizer", some will welcome it and most of us will fight it to the very end. As Mark Twain once said, "The fear of death follows from the fear of life. A man who lives fully is prepared to die at any time.

ABOUT THE AUTHOR

Sherri Brake grew up in NE Ohio with her family who had moved to the Buckeye state in one of the work migrations from West Virginia in the 1960's. Many summers, holidays and birthdays were spent in Webster County, West Virginia, visiting friends, grandparents, numerous aunts, uncles, and too many cousins to count. Storytelling of local lore and family tales were common in her family with many photographs and stories handed down through the generations. Her love of the mountains, its folklore, haunted locations, and ghost stories continues to grow with each year that passes.

Larry Brake, Sherri's father, was the family genealogist, historian and photographer, being the son of noted Webco Studio owner, the late Paul "Dutch" Brake. Sherri's father compiled and published several DVD productions on the history of Webster County, which were very well received. Sherri's mother, Suzi

(Green) Brake, was an unending source of many stories having grown up in the coal mining community of the Bergoo (Byers) area of Webster County.

Sherri lives in West Virginia on a farm in central West Virginia with her family. Her award winning tour company,
Haunted Heartland Tours, can be visited online at
www.HauntedHistory.net.
She welcomes stories of ghosts, odd happenings, folklore and haunted locations.

You can email the author at SherriBrake@gmail.com

ABOUT THE COVER

One of my favorite hobbies is photography. Foggy mist with shafts of sunlight is a wonder that I love to capture when possible. Fog in West Virginia seems to move, swirl and occasionally morphs into something both beautiful and sinister at the same time. This base image was taken in Randolph County, West Virginia and was put through a photographic filter for enhancement and colorization.

Stars on the map represent counties mentioned in this book,
Fireside Folklore of West Virginia Volume 4.

Clay County
Fayette County
Hardy County
Harrison County
Lewis County
Logan County
Mason County
Nicholas County
Pendleton County
Summers County
Tucker County
Upshur County
Webster County
Wood County

BOOKS BY THE AUTHOR

Haunted Stark County Ohio (2009)
The Haunted History of the Ohio State Reformatory (2010)
The Haunted History of the West Virginia Penitentiary (2011)
Fireside Folklore of West Virginia Vol. I (2012)
Fireside Folklore of West Virginia Vol. II (2014)
The Ghost Hunters Guide to the West Virginia Pen (2014)
The Haunted History of the Trans-Allegheny Lunatic Asylum (2014)
Fireside Folklore of West Virginia Vol. III (2017)

Visit the author's website to view tours, events,
ghost hunts and to order books
Haunted Heartland Tours
www.HauntedHistory.net

NOTES

39035279R00077

Made in the USA
Middletown, DE
17 March 2019